* * * * * * * * * * *

TRAITORS

* * * * * * * * * * * *

↠➤ By Virginia Loh-Hagan ◂✦

45TH PARALLEL PRESS

Published in the United States of America by Cherry Lake Publishing Group
Ann Arbor, Michigan
www.cherrylakepublishing.com

Reading Adviser: Beth Walker Gambro, MS, Ed., Reading Consultant, Yorkville, IL
Book Designer: Melinda Millward

Photo Credits: cover, title page: © Anneka/Shutterstock; page 7: © EnricoAliberti ItalyPhoto/Shutterstock; page 9: © Jorisvo/
Dreamstime.com; page 11: © ArtMari/Shutterstock; page 13: © FotoDuets/Shutterstock; page 12: © Mitotico/Shutterstock;
page 17: Francis Hayman, Public domain, via Wikimedia Commons; page 19: Blauvelt, Charles F., 1824-1900, artist, Public domain,
via Wikimedia Commons; page 20 (left): Thomas Hart, Public domain, via Wikimedia Commons; page 20 (right): Daniel Gardner,
Public domain, via Wikimedia Commons; page 23: Unidentified painter, Public domain, via Wikimedia Commons; page 25: History.
howstuffworks.com, Public domain, via Wikimedia Commons; page 27: Unknown author, Public domain, via Wikimedia Commons;
page 29: Roger Higgins, photographer from "New York World-Telegram and the Sun", Public domain, via Wikimedia Commons

Graphic Element Credits: Cover, multiple interior pages: © marekuliasz/Shutterstock,
© Andrey_Kuzmin/Shutterstock, © Here/Shutterstock

Library of Congress Cataloging-in-Publication Data has been filed and is available at catalog.loc.gov.

Cherry Lake Publishing Group would like to acknowledge the work of the Partnership for 21st Century Learning,
a Network of Battelle for Kids. Please visit http://www.battelleforkids.org/networks/p21 for more information.

Printed in the United States of America
Corporate Graphics

About the Author

Dr. Virginia Loh-Hagan is an author and educator. She is currently the Director of the Asian Pacific Islander Desi American
(APIDA) Center at San Diego State University and the Co-Executive Director of The Asian American Education Project. She lives
in San Diego with her very tall husband and very naughty dogs.

Note from publisher: Websites change regularly, and their future contents are outside of our control.
Supervise children when conducting any recommended online searches for extended learning opportunities.

TABLE OF CONTENTS

* * * * * * * * * * *

* * * * * * * * * * *

INTRODUCTION

* * * * * * * * * * *

Imagine **betraying** your country. Imagine betraying people you love. Traitors betray. They're not loyal. They sell out to the enemy. They spill top secrets. They commit **treason**. Treason is overthrowing one's government.

Traitors do shady things. They trick people. They lie. They mislead. They spy. They say one thing but do another. They gain people's trust. They use people.

Some traitors get caught. They miss details. They mix up lies. They make mistakes. They get called out. Some get sent to jail. Some get away. Learn about famous traitors in history.

★★★★★★★★★★★
CURRENT CASE:

A Reality Call

★ ★ ★ ★ ★ ★ ★ ★ ★

Reality Leigh Winner (born 1991) was in the U.S. Air Force. She had language training. She had intelligence training. Intelligence means information about threats. Winner had a high security clearance. She had access to top secrets. She left the U.S. Air Force. She worked for a company. Her job was to translate reports. She saw a top secret report. She stole it. The report was about Russia. It said Russia hacked the 2016 U.S. elections. Winner mailed it to *The Intercept*. *The Intercept* is a news website. It revealed Winner as the source.

Winner was caught. She was sent to jail. She was jailed for 5 years and 3 months. It's the longest jail time for such a crime. Winner said, "My actions were a cruel betrayal of my nation's trust in me."

MARCUS JUNIUS BRUTUS

(85–42 BCE)

Julius Caesar (100–44 BCE) was a Roman leader. Marcus Junius Brutus was friends with Caesar. Caesar upset many politicians. He became a tyrant. Tyrants are cruel leaders. They want power.

Brutus was a politician. He thought Caesar needed to be stopped. There was a **plot** to kill Caesar. Plot means plan. Brutus helped lead it. He wanted to save the Roman **republic**. Republics are governments elected by the people.

Caesar was stabbed 23 times. But Brutus's stab was

the most painful. He betrayed their friendship.

Two thousand years later, this betrayal lives on. William Shakespeare (1564–1616) was an English playwright. In a play, he wrote, "Et tu, Brute?" It means, "You too, Brutus?" These words are famous. They're used to question traitors.

Julius Caesar was killed on March 15. That day was called the Ides of March. Legend says Caesar was warned, "Beware the Ides of March."

JUDAS ISCARIOT

(3 BCE–30 CE)

Judas Iscariot was one of the 12 **apostles**. These men were the first followers of Jesus Christ (c. 4 BCE–30 CE). They taught his message. They supported him. They promoted him. They loved him. People who follow Jesus's teachings are called Christians.

Jesus was popular. He threatened officials. Iscariot told officials where Jesus was. He led them to him. He kissed him on the cheek. That's how officials identified Jesus. Jesus was arrested. Arrest means to take to jail.

Some say Iscariot did it for 30 pieces of silver. Others believe Jesus set him up. Jesus wanted Iscariot to betray him. This was part of God's plan. Jesus suffered. He was nailed to a cross. He died. But Christians believe he died to save humanity. They believe he came back to life. Iscariot's betrayal started it.

Judas Iscariot betrayed Jesus Christ in Jerusalem. They were in the Garden of Gethsemane.

BRITA TOTT
(1400s)

Brita Tott was Danish. She was a **noble**. Nobles are from a high class. Her family owned lands. They had power. Tott married a Swedish nobleman.

A war broke between Sweden and Denmark (1451–1452). Tott lived in Sweden. But she helped Denmark. She wrote to the Swedish king's enemies. She plotted to kill him. She wrote to the Danes. She gave them Swedish war plans. Tott also faked papers. She illegally sold Swedish lands to the Danes.

Tott was caught in 1452. The Swedes charged her with treason. They wanted to burn her at the stake. But Tott was held in a **priory** instead. A priory is run by monks and nuns. Tott had to pay the church. She paid for paintings for the church. She included a picture of herself.

Brita Tott wrote to the Swedish king's enemies during the war between Sweden and Denmark from 1451 to 1452.

GUY FAWKES
(1570–1606)

King James I (1566–1625) ruled England. He banished Catholic priests. This upset many people. Catholic nobles were upset. They plotted in 1605. They got 36 barrels. The barrels had gunpowder. They were placed under **Westminster**. Westminster is a palace. It is where the English government meets. There was a meeting of leaders. The king was there. Many would have died. But the Gunpowder Plot was stopped.

Guy Fawkes was a soldier. He was next to the barrels. He had matches. His job was to light the gunpowder. But he was caught. He gave up names. The plotters were punished. Their crime was treason.

November 5 is Guy Fawkes Day. It's a night of bonfires. It's a night of fireworks. It celebrates a failed **assassination**. Assassination is the killing of a public person.

The plotters swore an oath of secrecy.
They swore on a prayer book.

A Guy Fawkes figure is burned on bonfire night in England.

There is a famous folk song and nursery rhyme about it.

Remember, remember the Fifth of November,
The Gunpowder Treason and Plot,
I know of no reason
Why the Gunpowder Treason
Should ever be forgot.

COLD CASE:

The Unsolved Mystery of Ashraf Marwan

* * * * * * * * * *

Ashraf Marwan (1944–2007) was from Egypt. He was a billionaire. He was a spy for Israeli intelligence. His code name was "the Angel." He was married to the Egyptian president's daughter. He worked in the president's office. He had access to top secrets. He leaked war plans. He leaked meeting notes. He shared private talks. Some say he was a double agent. They say he was giving the Israeli government false information. They say he spied for both countries. They say he gave fake information. They say he misled people on purpose. But this could be a cover-up. He died in 2007. He was in London. He was in his apartment. He fell from the balcony. He fell 5 stories. Police lost his shoes. His shoes may have proven if he was pushed. Some people think he was killed. No one knows for sure.

* * * * * * * * * * *

MIR JAFAR

(c. 1691–1765)

* * * * * * * * * * *

Mir Jafar betrayed India. He was a general. He led an army. Indians were fighting the British. The Battle of Plassey was fought in 1757. Jafar switched sides. He made an agreement with the British. The British only had 3,000 men. The Indians had 50,000 men. Jafar held his forces back. He let the British win. He also planned his daughter's marriage. He married her to a British governor.

The battle was important. The British took control over eastern India. Over the years, they controlled the rest of India.

Jafar helped end the Mughal Empire. He wanted more power. He wanted money. He saw more opportunities with the British. People say "mirjafar" or "meer jafar." His name is used to talk about traitors.

Mir Jafar was a general in the Indian army. He made an agreement with the British to let them win in the Battle of Plassey.

* * * * * * * * * * *
BENEDICT ARNOLD
(1741–1801) AND
PEGGY SHIPPEN
(1760–1804)
* * * * * * * * * * *

Americans wanted to be free from British rule. Benedict Arnold fought in the American Army. He became a major general.

Arnold married Margaret "Peggy" Shippen in 1779. Her family was rich. They were loyal to Britain. Shippen was friends with John André (1751–1780). André was a British officer.

Arnold switched sides. He passed secret messages. He shared war plans. He sent them to Shippen. Shippen sent them to André.

Arnold plotted to **surrender** West Point. Surrender means to give up. West Point was a military fort. Arnold took command of West Point. He weakened it. He stopped repairs. He drained supplies.

American forces captured André. André was hanged.

Benedict Arnold passed secret messages to Margaret "Peggy" Shippen. She passed them along to John André.

Benedict Arnold (left) and Margaret "Peggy" Shippen (right)

Arnold ran away. Shippen faked an emotional break-down. She stalled the arresting officers. She gave Arnold time to get away. He fled to a British ship. He was made a British general. He led raids.

Americans won the war. They hated Arnold. Arnold moved to London. The British blamed him for André's death. Arnold moved to Canada. Canadians burned a statue of him. He died in debt. His name is famous. Americans remember his betrayal.

WORST-CASE SCENARIO:

A Big Betrayal

＊ ＊ ＊ ＊ ＊ ＊ ＊ ＊ ＊ ＊

Alfred Redl (1864–1913) was born in Austria. He wanted to be a nobleman. His family was poor. He joined the army. He rose in the ranks. He went to school. He studied Russian military issues. He became an officer. He led the intelligence office. He improved its methods. He used cameras. He used recording devices. He created a system for fingerprint records. He impressed people. But he was also a spy. He received money from Russia. He helped Russia. He was their leading spy. He gave Russia war plans. He shared military secrets. He sent agents to their deaths in Russia. He gave fake news to his own government. His actions hurt his own country. They led to the deaths of half a million people. He's known as one of history's greatest traitors.

✳✳✳✳✳✳✳✳✳✳✳
MAGDALENA RUDENSCHOLD
(1766–1823)
✳✳✳✳✳✳✳✳✳✳✳

Magdalena Rudenschold was a Swedish countess. She was in the royal court. She served the king's sister. She was pretty. She was lively. She had many fans.

She fell in love with Gustaf Mauritz Armfelt (1757–1814). Armfelt was the king's closest adviser. The king was killed. The new king was only 14. His uncle became the **regent**. Regents rule until rulers become old enough.

Armfelt was denied a position. He left Sweden. He plotted. He wanted to rule Sweden himself. He wrote to Rudenschold. He drew her into the plot. He wanted to overthrow the regent. He wanted to get Russian support.

Rudenschold helped Armfelt. She spied for him. She tried to win over the young Swedish king. She wanted him to support the overthrow plot. The young king stayed loyal to the regent. Rudenschold was arrested. She committed treason for love.

Magdalena Rudenschold was a Swedish countess in the royal court. She committed treason for love.

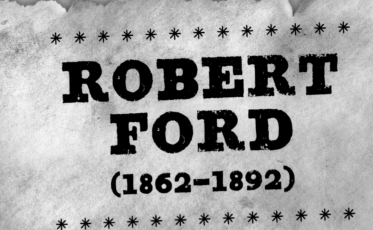

* * * * * * * * * * * * *

ROBERT FORD

(1862–1892)

* * * * * * * * * * * * *

Robert Ford is known for killing Jesse James (1847–1882). He did this in 1882. He was in James's gang. They were American **outlaws**. Outlaws are people who break the law. They robbed banks. They robbed trains.

Ford was caught in an illegal act. The sheriff made a deal with him. He said he'd pardon him. He just had to kill James. Ford agreed. James was a wanted man. There was a $10,000 **bounty** for James. Bounty means a sum paid for capturing someone.

James was cleaning a dusty picture. Ford drew his gun. He shot. He hit the back of James's head. He called the sheriff. He didn't get a reward. Instead, he was arrested for murder. But he didn't serve any jail time.

People called Ford a traitor. He was also called a "dirty little coward."

Multiple drawings were made of what Robert Ford said happened when he shot Jesse James.

WANG JINGWEI
(1883–1944)

The Second **Sino**-Japanese War was from 1937 to 1945. Sino means Chinese. Japan wanted to expand. They attacked China. China resisted.

Wang Jingwei was Chinese. He held high government positions. He worked with Japan. He did this in 1938. He disobeyed orders. China wanted to fight. Wang wanted peace. He signed a **treaty** with Japan. Treaty means an agreement.

Japan formed a government in Nanking. Nanking is in eastern China. Japan made Jingwei head of state. It was a Japanese **puppet government**. It was really ruled by Japan. Wang took orders from Japan.

Wang died in Japan. He was not loved by the Chinese. Some think he was poisoned.

Wang Jingwei was Chinese, but became head of a Japanese puppet government in Nanking, China.

* * * * * * * * * * * *
JULIUS (1918-1952) AND
ETHEL (1915-1952)
ROSENBERG
* * * * * * * * * * * *

Julius and Ethel Rosenberg were Americans. They were spies. They helped the Soviet Union. This country no longer exists. It consisted of Russia and several smaller countries. Julius was an engineer. He worked for the U.S. Army. Ethel was his assistant.

They shared top secrets. They shared many reports. They reported on **radar**. They reported on **sonar**. Radar and sonar are waves. These waves are used to detect things. The Rosenbergs also reported on **atomic** bombs. These bombs use powerful energy. They're deadly. They were used to end World War II (1939–1945).

The Rosenbergs were caught in 1951. They denied doing anything wrong. They were found guilty. They were put to death. They died in the electric chair. They are the only Americans executed for spying during peacetime.

During this time, people were scared. They feared communism. Some people thought the Rosenbergs were unfairly targeted.

FOR YOUR EYES ONLY...

* * * * * * * * * *

HOW TO BE A TRAITOR!*

Do you want to be a traitor? Do you have what it takes? Here are 3 tips:

Tip #1: Collect information.

Get a job with access to top secrets. Get information. Meet important people. Make connections. Get people to trust you.

Tip #2: Work under pressure.

Manage stress. There's a chance you'll get caught. People will doubt you. They will accuse you. Learn to be calm. Learn to **deflect**. Deflect means to distract.

Tip #3: Hide in plain sight.

Avoid attention. Fit in. Don't stand out. Don't sneak around either. Act like you belong.

*WARNING: Traitors can go to jail. They can hurt their country. Don't be a traitor.

ICYW: IN CASE YOU'RE WONDERING...

The Science Behind Betrayal

* * * * * * * * * * *

Betrayal destroys trust. It makes people question themselves. It breaks their confidence. So why do people betray? Some people are greedy. They'll do anything to get what they want. They are easily tempted. Some people hurt one person to save another. Some people betray to prove they're smart. They like to play with people's minds. They like to stir up trouble.

Sigmund Freud (1856–1939) studied the mind. He thinks trust depends on mothers. If mothers care for their babies, then they will have trust. Some scientists think betrayal is why people moved around the world. Around 100,000 years ago, people formed communities. Some started to lie and cheat. This forced people to move away from their enemies. They wanted to avoid betrayal.

GLOSSARY

apostles (uh-PAH-suhls) the first followers of Jesus Christ

assassination (uh-sah-suh-NAY-shuhn) murder by sudden or secret attack, often for political reasons

atomic (uh-TAH-mik) relating to the rapid release of nuclear energy

betraying (bih-TRAY-ing) delivering to an enemy by treachery

bounty (BOUN-tee) a sum paid for capturing someone

deflect (dih-FLEKT) to distract or turn away

noble (NOH-buhl) person of a high rank in society, especially in Europe

outlaws (OWT-lawz) a person who breaks the law and is on the run

plot (PLAHT) a secret plan

priory (PRY-uh-ree) a religious house led by monks or nuns

puppet government (PUH-puht GUH-vuhr-muhnt) a government that appears to have authority but is really controlled by another power

radar (RAY-dahr) detection using radio waves through the air

regent (REE-juhnt) a person who governs a kingdom if the sovereign is too young or not able to serve

republic (rih-PUH-blik) a government that is elected by its citizens

Sino (sye-NOH) relating to China

sonar (SOH-nahr) detection using sound waves in water

surrender (suh-REHN-duhr) to give up

treason (TREE-zuhn) the crime of betraying one's country

treaty (TREE-tee) a pact or agreement between two or more parties

Westminster (WEST-min-ster) a palace in London, England, where the British government and Houses of Parliament do business

LEARN MORE!

Burgan, Michael. *Spies and Traitors: Stories of Masters of Deception*. North Mankato, MN: Capstone Press, 2010.

Landau, Elaine. *Assassins, Traitors, and Spies*. Minneapolis, MN: Lerner Publications, 2017.

Lawrence, Sandra. *Hideous History: Trials and Trickery*. New York, NY: Little Bee Books, 2016.

Mitchell, Susan K. *Spies, Double Agents, and Traitors*. Berkely Heights, NJ: Enslow Publishing, 2012.

INDEX